Beneath the surface

Beneath the surface

To Voyagers, Dark Souls and Dreamers

THOUGHTS

IN COSMOS

Pulse
the creator of the universes
necessity of being

different physic-laws of the universes
physics and coincidence
confusers of the space

sources of life, the spiral galaxies
death-rays of the supernova
the cosmic ocean of life and death
the riddle of spiral

I'm a thinker, free thinker
not believer...but still I believe...in greater forces
there's got to be something...
in the star-idea bubble-incubator

...

I ride a comet
I'm in a flyby and I'm just scratching the surface
time flies, time teaches
light seeks

are we connected to each other in the multiversum?
Different versions of everything
different versions...of me

friendly whales are swimming towards me
whales are staring at me and they communicate telepathically:
"the bigger you are, the faster time goes...and the smaller...more slowly
time is relative
all living is one
yoga"

observing eyes of eternal night
eyes of investigator
eyes of the superior creature proceed monitoring...

far away...

in the infinity

LORD

Unstoppable time
destruction, reincarnation
circulation...
over and over again

lost species, new species
survival instinct has kept us alive...
for now

the time, the Lord, the creator, the terminator
the artist runs the show
evolution waits for no one nor nothing

the endless universe, the strange events...
makes me wonder the miracles

the processes, the prophecies...
will proceed...
for now

CHOICE

God already exists?
Do you want to replace it?
No
so...
face it

"life is a scene, play it well,...
if you dont, you end up in hell"
they may say so,...
but you`re in the main role
think outside of the box
morality is a fox

you know what's right...?

- *"Conan!*
What is best in life?"
- *"To crush your enemies, see them driven before you, and to hear the*
lamentations of their women!"
- *"That is good!"*
My soul food

what is my life mission?
Is there such?
Have I already fullfilled it?
It confuses me much
will it ever be full-...
enough?
Shut the fuck up!

Comprehend
develop
help others
love comes back to you...
fucker

unexplorated are the ways...
of the God-particles
find yourself...
in the mystery-...
articles

the choice is yours

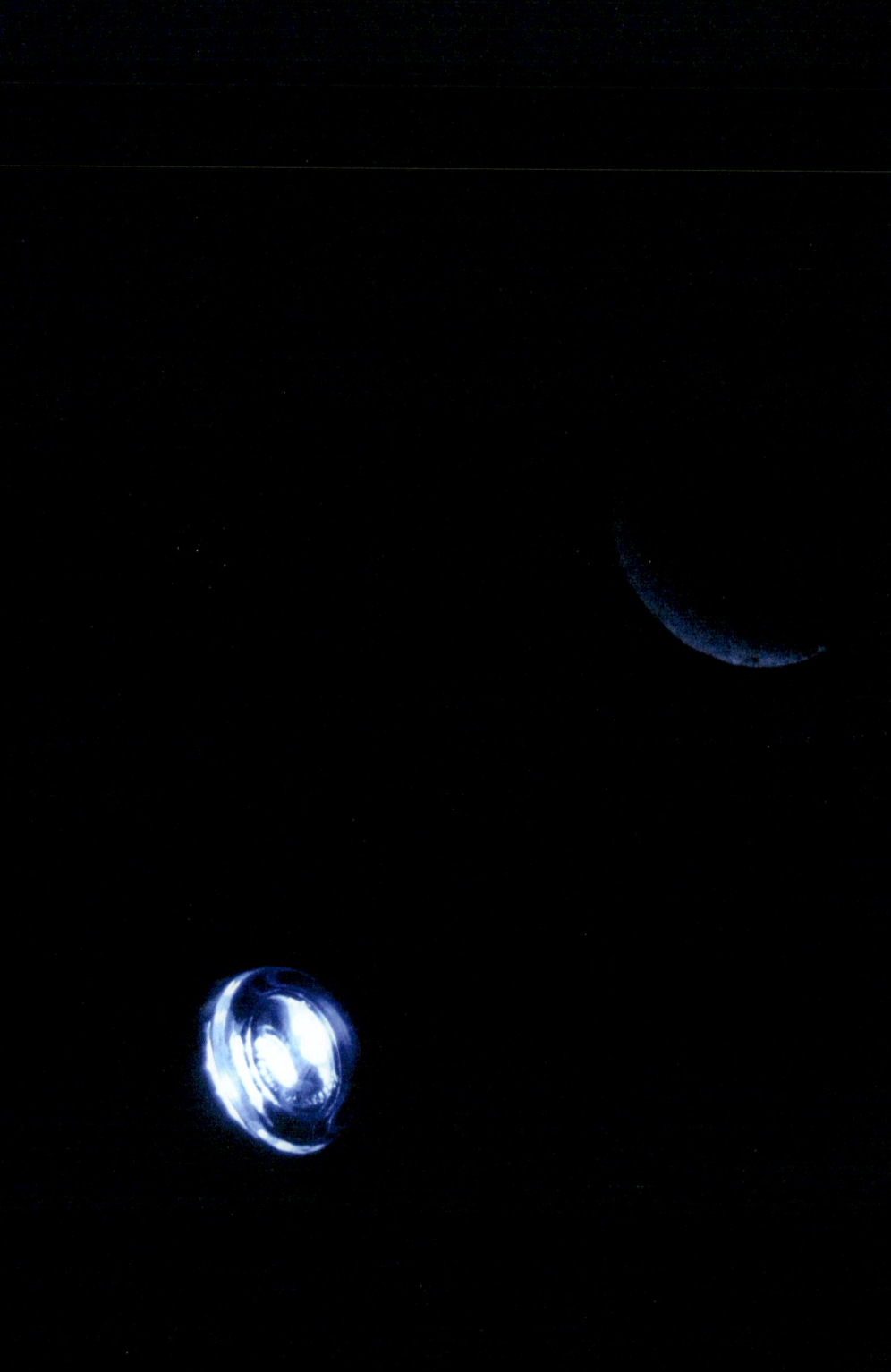

THE OMNISCIENT

I am

space
silence
cold darkness
fear and emptiness
eternity

one and all

inexplicable things, madness
miraculousness…
mixing into the fantasy dream

I'm a whale
diving, sinking down…
into insanity…
in a ball pit of loneliness

unreal visions, states, aphorisms
souls, spirits, energys
spirals…
in the unquenchable vortex of cosmos…
creating continuum of existence…
purpose?

Endless blur of time
mysticism...
leads to another time

I am…

I'm a creature...

The Omniscient

OBSERVERS

Wakeful eyes have seen into the beginning of time
billions of light years away
into the time before galaxies

wakeful eyes have seen into the big bang and Its afterglow
into the reddish shine and following particles

cosmic background radiation reveals and tells a story of the reason-
light from the past
It proceeds and heads into the future, into the supervention

limitless coincidences of time
organic matter
microbes in rocks are spreading still wider into the space
there is life everywhere

...

dark energy is expanding the consciousness in accelerating speed
wakeful eyes are seeing still further

black holes inside of the black holes
come from destruction and go into the destruction

we are stardust...

in a void

FINDIAN

In the psychedelic iced-landscape...
the northern lights are painting nuances into the pastel-skies shape
in the horizon, force majeure
lonely findian in his bearfur is looking into the future
beneath the Fin'...
bare-backed horse is blowing off steam in its nostrils

the winds of change are getting stronger and soughing the feathers of
the shamans headwear
wind starts to whistle and the icy storm is on its way here
the half-breed senses the upcoming, he sees into the wisdom
winds are blowing a new era into the kingdom

tribal-drums are rumbling rhythm in a faraway lands
the sky and the space are starting to fill up with symbols
the supernatural is making wolfes to howl
magical moment stops the seer-owl

it is the beginning of something bigger
all the symbols are pointing into the omen
the visions showed it
the stones told it

the forest and the swamp are calling
Findian disappears, symbols are fading
the spirit animal answers the call
smoke signals are guiding their own

the Findian, the nature, and the spirit of the magical firefox
the survivor, the invincible force, and the guardian rocks...
in the holy union...

in the wilderness of time and eternity

SHAPE-SHIFTER

In a peaceful primeval forest...
you are the survivor, the guest
perspective atmosphere...
and fear
realness
magical spellness
heart-warming beauty of nature
so nude, virgin immature
harmonic oscillator

the shape-shifter is croaking and calling a soulmate day in, day out
the forest answers with mysterious silence...day in, day out
some will hear the call...
but not soulmates of this fall

the wait is long and melancholic
poem symphonic
shape symbolic
heart-breaking and sad
cold, suffering and mad
there's just fog and silence
twisted mental violence
no one's there...
and I'm elsewhere

the longing is reflecting from the eyes...
but the hope's beginning to end likewise
the mirror of the soul doesn't lie
there's no promise of comfort to find
starting to get used to the pain of my heart and my mind
it is making me blind

dark shadows are getting longer
the exhaustion of life causes to fall into a deep sleep stronger
the night entwines into the pitch-black embrace
it swallows you into the kingdom of dark-haze...
into the endless maze

the moon keeps an eye on the night...
and the dark souls of the might
the moon, the sun is the only light...
that can create this poetry-like, dreamlike sight

there's just something...that cannot be phrased
forest is a place where everyone can confront themselves...
face to face...

naturally

IN THE GRAVEYARD

We're walking slowly in the graveyard
nature is death-silent
we're walking with our thoughts
peacefulness is giving us time to think
it stops us

my old Turkish friend is mumbling prayers in Turk
I'm listening and thinking, I'm giving him peace
the great unknown makes a man silent and humble, makes him
respect...
makes him serious

my friend starts to talk about life...
and its injustice
its wrongness, which is hard to deal with

we understand each other

time doesn't wait or empathize
winter brings the death
I feel the cold exitus chilling my bones
nature is taking it's own

the smoke of the crematorium reminds us of our limited time and
circuit life
the fragility of life

death restoring us back to the nature...
back into the soil

snow covers the sorrow...
but the memories will follow...us...

to our end

PERKELE

You...

You lit my heart
into fire You lit it
to burn hate
to fight

the beast is raging and roaring in my mind
blind fury is rising and it wants to get unleashed...
to blast and to destroy all the light
to rule the eternal night

...

blow me into the kill
blow me into the ash and smoke...
into the peace of mind and hope...
into the dope

light no more candles...
candles of black
paint no more ugly picture
find where your at

You...
my inner friend...

my Perkele

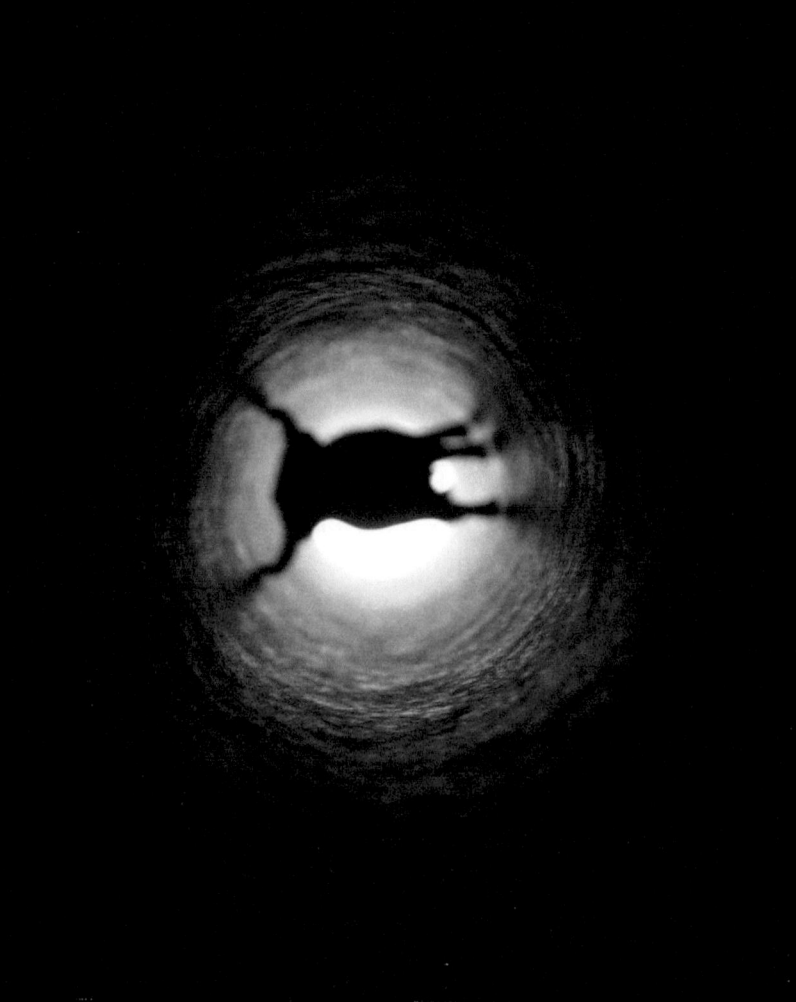

MINOTAUROS HORRORSCOPE

I see red
I see my enemy who is bullying me
I'm focusing my horns towards my enemy
I will destroy you eventually

my senses are sharping into attack
my mind is blurring into indiscriminate rage
the blood's roaring into rampage
I attack

the enemy is bluffing me and sticks a dagger into my nape
I'm weakening
I try to attack again
the enemy is bluffing me again and sticks another dagger into my nape
I'm weakening old
starting to feel cold

I'm trying with my final strenght to attack into my hated one
again I get a dagger into my nape
I'm full of hate
I'm out of energy and getting frustrated
the final dagger drops me to end it

...

the blood of the futility has been bloodshed again...
and the foolish folk celebrates the violent and cruel winner-idiot

barbarianism

when do we learn and change?

Senseless bullshit

idiocy

WEIRDO

Jazz fills my mind
I'm the weird kind
I am and I'm thinking, I want to be
I'm not complete

I write, I paint, I photograph and I play drums
alone I get lost into the forest fungus
nothing works...or is working
I have to invent something

I'm travelling and I'm seeking inspiration from the edge of the world
all the way through the universal harmonic chord
the experiences are bringing depth and content into the life
still once in a while, I get bored, something's missing though

I don't get fullfillment as such
do I insist too much?
Feel so hollow
into the unknown future it will follow

I climbed to the top of my pyramid to look at the sky where it ends
the bubbles of dreams are bursting and waking me up where the
surreality bends
I get a connection into the life again...
but do I really want that in vain?

...

It's time to take seriously life itself
must get a grip on myself
how boring it is...well...
so boring...it is hell!

"The weird role" of an artist, the role of the madman stays on...
but on the other hand it doesn't matter, I play along
no shame, nothing to loose
I belong nowhere, do I have to choose?

I'm looking and I'm waiting for the signs
I'm looking for comprehension of minds
will I find my hole, my shelter, in this storm?
Among all the hellish mayhem perform

still I have the energy to wish...
even when I'm lost sometimes in skirmish
will my divergent find my identity...
and make me a complete human being in my entity?

May destiny show my way
maybe I will find my space...
my home, my grace
It's not easy to be a different face

it's a real haze-maze

JOKER

When I was searching for my own essence I had to get through all the roles
I play normal or abnormal role, or actually I'm not even playing...so...
the roles of my own are not dead, the role models are dead
I'm protecting my own sensitive inner self, I'm hiding behind my roles
so...fuck it!

There's two sides of me
I cannot introduce myself with my own name you see
insecurity, concentration disorder, anxiety, cross-melodies
I cannot describe my monstrous state of being
psychological sweat indeed

maybe my personality is changing when I get angry, but why?
I'm searching the right way, direction and comprehension from the signs
I'm trying to find the wisdoms of life
who am I?

I grew apart from myself
I was living a frustrated grey life in spiritually high
I didn't find comprehension...
until I had to confront my true self mind

I stopped...to think
what do I like...for real?
I was listening to my heart and my soul
I was focusing to do the real things...so...
the only and the right way to live is to forgive...oh!

I don't care anymore about the opinions of others, I'm doing my own story
I'm real, original, unique...individual glory
I don't fake my life
no remorse when I'm old horse in high

the moment in the smoke
my home is my prison, my hole
I'm a fool and a wizard
must find the inner main being, the lizard

I escape into my writings
I could be a king if I want to
I'm not sure if I want to
I could be anything, I'm not a convict of my image
I'm the thing

I'm frustrated, tired
the bulwarks of the people, masks must be destroyed
the truth will be discovered from the inner space, from the void

my superior me, my cosmic consciousness
my inferior me, my ego, my masks, my roles
these cards were dealt, with these we go on
adamant mind goes through the grey stone

I'm a semi-depressed working-class hippie artist
introvert village idiot, OCD, HSP
I'm trying to be me...
myself and I
you'll see

EXPERIENCES

SUICIDE MONDAY

My co-worker didn't come to work today
he hanged himself away
I knew him for a week
he had more serious problems than I had, indeed

hangover and shitwork didn't bother me much
everybody was in the deep thoughts
everybody was thinking about the reason
he was just so young to pass on

he had been working only for one week
the work didn't really interest him, you see
the working looked phlegmatic
he wasn't attached in the moment, he was in panic

the announcement and the silent moment were arranged at noon
people were pretty upset the whole afternoon
the day continued peacefully and emphatically
it was a pretty quiet day, so sorry

life goes on...
to others

death harvests the inconsolable brothers

POETRY-LIKE WAIT

The day is cold and wintry
I'm intoxicated and I'm waiting for sleep instinctively
tears watering my eyes...cause of tiredness
I'm in my thoughts, my highness

in the kitchen, the drops of the leaking tap are falling into the plate
and breaking the silence
the drops inducing sound like an eastern bell guidance
it creates a specially peaceful atmosphere,
almost like a spiritual feeling near
a moment of stagnation, a holy creation

I'm in my spellbounds
I'm in my poems

ready for dreamzone

THE DREAMZONE

In the darkness I'm lying with my eyes closed
thoughts are transforming into colourful shapes, fictional voices within
endless abyss of imagination...
taken by the emotions, dominating feelings
peaceful mind wandering, exploring, inventing, experiencing
pleasant journey desires for enjoyment

lazy focus skips the limits of awareness
mind control is out of reach
senseless revolution, eternity of existence
no self-distance

beyond consciousness, my mind is setting free and achieves nirvana
the final destination

absolute perfection

conception

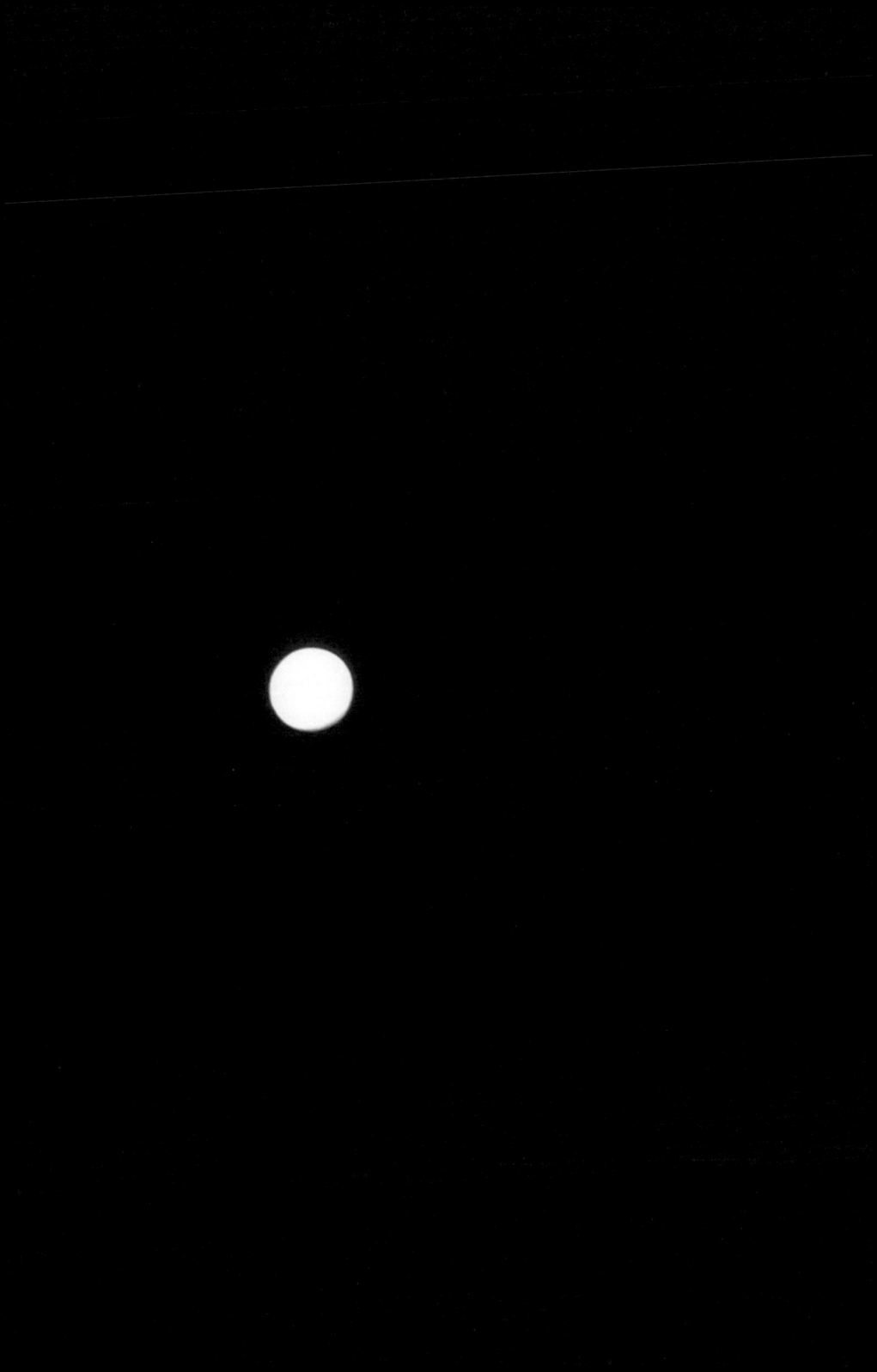

BEASTS OF THE NIGHT

I sleep with the beasts almost every night
tenseness is intense
present every night
the beasts are lurking...
watching...
waiting for fight

there's just darkness...
senses...
instinct...
and fear
making it all so clear
the skirmish is near

sharp claws are scratching
a glimpse of grey
the beasts are preparing...
to prey

the eyes are shining, staring from the darkness
sharp mauling-teeth are projecting
the beasts are hissing like aliens...
bloodthirsty
ready to attack
ready to kill
...
cats are cute...
for real

("purr...")

NOT MY CUP OF TEA

I wake up when someone is knocking on my door
It's a hot summer morning and I've got a horrible hangover overall
the knocking continues...- who the fuck is it?
Head confused I step into the hall and I open the door

the drunken couple from the neighbour
the woman is staring at me and she says: "your cat came to our balcony
and then it fell down"
drunken Mr. Hakkarainen proceeds: "yeah there it thumped...it's dead"
- "oh fuck...I put my clothes on"
I close the door and my heart is throbbing to the floor
have I fucked up?

I put my clothes on quickly and a mistake I notice
the balcony glass is open, I close it
one forgotten thing is enough
it's 07.00. am and it's friday morning
I check the cats
Kylli...Ninja is missing...fuck!

I pray in my mind: "be a Ninja...survive",
when I ran downstairs to the backyard
Mr. Hakkarainen is waiting there and he says: "here it thumped...
can't see it"
I look into the neighbours balcony and there it is under the chair
it's meowing afraid and doesn't dare to move a hair
- phew...it's alive...and well

I jump to the side of the balcony and I'm luring Ninja to come to me
at first it hesitates, then it dares to come to me
I'm petting to calm it and I'm lifting it up to my lap

gums are little bit bloody but otherwise it seems to be alright
the cat is shaking, no wonder that

I'm lifting up the cat over the rail of the balcony
and I drop it to its feet
it seems to be alright, it is in tend indeed
I'm also climbing over the rail and I'm taking the cat into my lap
the neighbour comes out into the balcony and wonders what the hell is
going on out here
I'm explaining the situation and everything is alright with the cat

I'm carring Ninja back inside into the hallway and it's clawing me
frightened all the way
scratching doesn't bother me much in this situation as such...
where Mr. Hakkarainen is going home, I thank and I'm going home too
- phew...fuck
the cats are wondering to each other for a while until everything is
back to normal line
I'm going straight into the shower to get a heart attack in hangover

Thank God that Ninja is alive and didn't get injured
it fell three floors down and survived...only startled
a true Ninja warrior

all's well that ends well

maybe everybody learned something...
or maybe not
either way...
but not forgetting...
that hangover I had

- fuck!

THE MOMENT

In the darkness, I find myself again on the sofa
melancholic piano is tolling on TV, alone like a coma
on the bookshelf, cats are cleaning each other in harmony
loneliness detected heavily

house wine is chugging in the closet and It's killing me slowly
It reminds me of my condition and my death reality
the time, the moment, my world has stopped
I'm numb

black clouds are casting shadows over me
I'm too tired of grieving, too tired of being depressed
dead tired living being

is there any point in all of this?

...

Yes...

there always is

I have no energy to think
time to sink

the melancholic piano is colouring me into the lonely dream...
into the lonely space

beautiful darkness...haze...

I'm yours

LONER

I'm drowning into the darkness in a chosen bubble of loneliness
wrong thoughts are leading me into destruction
I'm encapsulating into my own pain, into my own shadow
coldness has got me

I'm like a moon, alone...in a darkness
I have lived my life half in melancholy, in the emptiness
something died in me already a long time ago
I don't recognise myself anymore

I'm losing myself, I'm changing
I'm air, I'm fading
apocalypse of emotions
slow motion oceans
is there a reason to live?
Do I have something to give?

No comfort, nowhere sun, darkness follows me everywhere I run
there is no help, I know that, and I wouldn't even want that
irritation, suffering, depression, sadness...hell
It can only be accepted as well

after days of laying I'm starting to feel like my muscles are atrophying
hunger sores my stomach and my head hurts almost into vomit
I'm not interested to get up from my bed
I would just like to sleep all the time into the end

the only reason to get up from my bed is to feed my cats, my guardians
modern time human enslavers know what to do with the depressed ones
they wake me up and protect me...
from myself

life is a tragedy that doesn't end happily
It's difficult to define and put suffering into perspective
time saves and tortures...endlessly

loneliness is like a poetry of pain
dark and blue, beautiful rain
real and eternal like
peaceful but powerful, it keeps holding tight…
like a lurking night

I try to create myself again but I think it's too late
I cannot fix everything, okay?
I want to forgot and hide
I want to fall asleep and die

rain is drumming me into asleep so fine

dreamworld changes the depressed mind

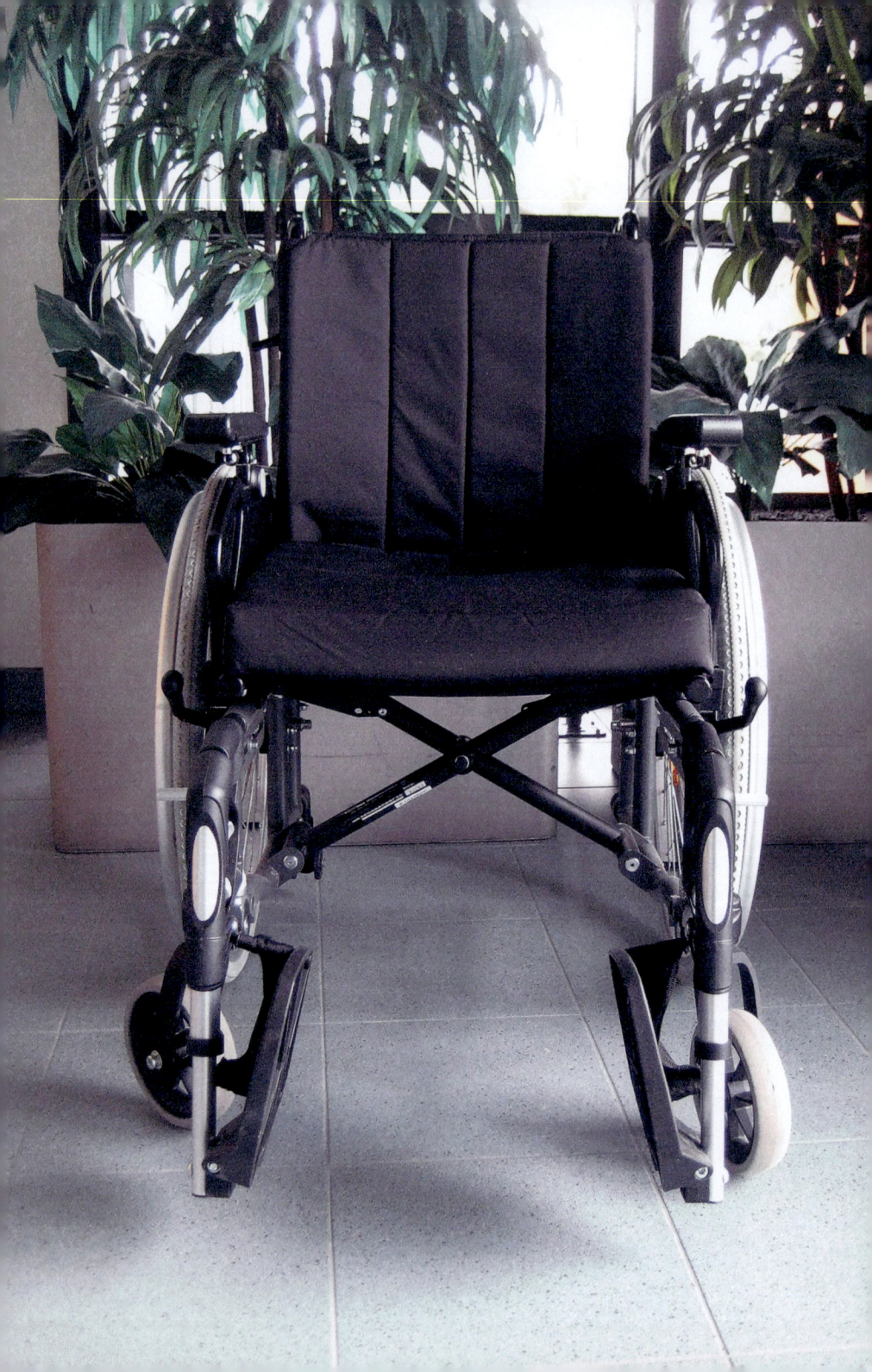

PAROXYSM (Nephrolithiasis)

- Pain

waving pain is keeping me awake
what is this?
The pain continues
it's getting worse

the pain is getting unbearable
- what the fuck?!
Panic attacks
my pulse is rising and my breath accelerating
- what is happening to me?!

pain is making me vomit, cold sweat pouring from my head
my limbs are starting to get numb, my eyes are starting to get blurry
I call to emergency help
come and get me
...

paramedics are taking me into the ambulance by wheelchair
still I have to blow to the alcohol meter
- fuck, what else?!
...

In the hospital, I'm screaming pain
the nurse is giving opioids to me
relief

after a while the pain returns
more opioids
relief

but the pain won't stop
more...

finally after about ten shots, I'm full of opioids
the nurse is pushing me in a hospital-bed and wondering how can I
still be in my right mind
I'm just reliefed
I'm arriving into a pale room
nurses are shooting me with different kind of equipments
the reason for the pain can't be found
...

in the morning, they let me go home...
to medicine treatment...
to wait

MR. HAKKARAINEN A.K.A. "THE SHOVEL MAN"

Monday 11:00
I wake up, I put Diabolus in Musica record on and I have to take a shit
my neighbor Mr. Hakkarainen starts to kick my outdoor and I cannot
take a peaceful shit
- soon he will come through the door? Should I wipe already?
a thought...
anyway I end my shit and I'm listening when he's raging and cursing it
- I think he's not into Slayer any bit
after the shit I turn down the music before he goes totally nuts
I start to make breakfast

Tuesday 16:30
I start to play electric drums with my headphones on and still I hear
that mr. Hakkarainen is going mad-zone
I hear cursing and stomping when he opens his door and shouts:
"GODDAMN MOTHERFUCKER!"
I'll wait for a moment until he closes his door, then I play more
mr. Hakkarainen opens his door again and shouts: "SON OF A
BITCH! WHO IS IT?!"
He starts to kick every door of the apartment house cause he obviously
doesn't know where the "noise" is coming from
doormats are flying when he's raging and rumbling...
until he goes back to his home
I try to play one more time for a test
he comes to the door and shouts his best: "GODDAMNIT! BOOM
BOOM BOOM BOOM!"

He leaves the door open, then moves his stereo to the hall and puts the
radio at maximum volume
then he comes to the hallway with somekind of jingle bells in his hands
and starts to jingle them
maybe I must quit playing...with him

Wednesday 18:00
I hear that mr. Hakkarainen is beating his woman again and doing
God knows what
his door opens and he comes to the hallway au naturel, what a fuck
I'm watching from the eyehole of my door when he's kicking madly the
neighbors door
he shouts: "GODDAMNIT! I KILL! I KILL!", and he's shaking his fist
then he goes back to his apartment and slams the door to close it
arguing and fighting continues, what a fucking shit

Thursday 19:00
I hear fighting from the neighbor again and the woman screams:
"STOP STRANGLING ME!"
I call the cops cause it starts to sound so worrying indeed
It takes 15 minutes for the cops to get in here and the women makes an
escape from the apartment
from the chink of the door, I give a hint to the cops of what has
happened
the cops are ringing the door bell and knocking but mr. Hakkarainen
doesn't open the door
cops are leaving and I'm amazed once more

Friday 15:00
I'm coming home and I see an ambulance in the yard
I guess it's Hakkarainen coming in hard
- what this time?
I'm going home and I hear that the paramedics are at his apartment at
the time
the woman was having a seizure, I heard afterwards
- sure thing, sarcastic applause
...
Even after that nothing changed here
same hell continued as long as they lived there
according to the latest news mr. Hakkarainen has been seen digging a
hole in the ditch
- sure he wasn't at work, maybe he was digging a grave for his bitch...
but I hope rather to himself
in his previous residence mr. Hakkarainen hit the neighbor in the head
with a shovel, result of an argument
what an ace, what an accident

- mr. Hakkarainen...
the shovel man
what a fucking idiot

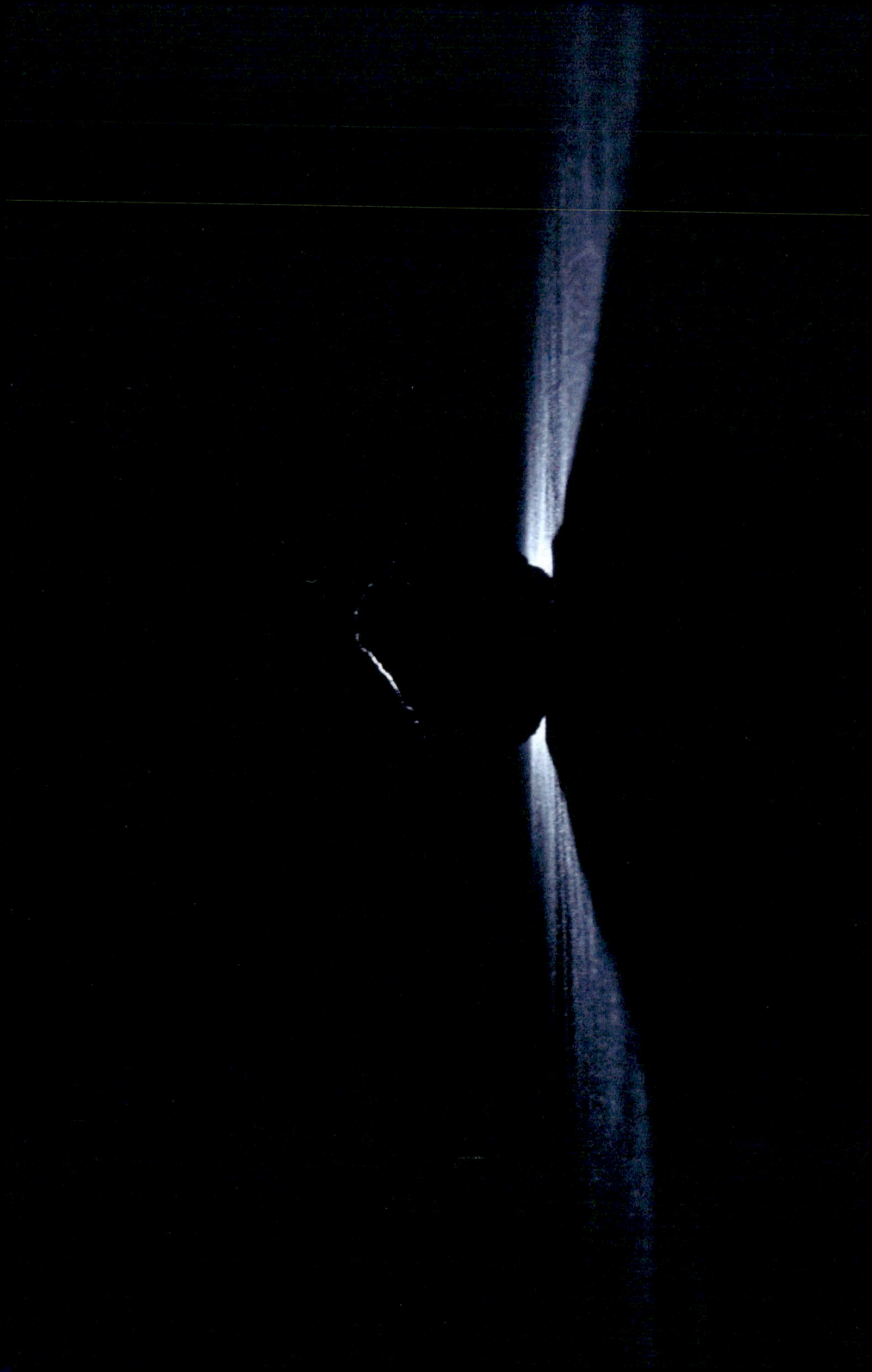

MAGIC LIMIT

A fickle line where the fear and the curiosity come across
a line where the other side, the darkside begins
the deep where you can drown

unknown zone
inexplicableness or madness
interesting but scary space...
that mind may not be able to process

there the sky is not the limit
there are no limits at all
there's just hyper-connections and restless creativity

One cannot be sure to ever return once there?
Can one ever be ready to face it?
Should we be afraid of our own thoughts?
Can we handle or control the insanity?

It can be hard to hide the inner ghosts if they are to appear
they can be scary
you could frighten yourself...
lose yourself

...

when you are experiencing the new world, remember the old one
remember who you are
remember the basics of life

control your mind
you could learn to understand

GHOST

Sometimes when I'm lying on my bed with my eyes closed and waiting
for sleep…
I feel that something is snuggling into my bed
I stop breathing and I stay alert
I feel that something is touching my bed and it's not my cat
when I look, I don't see anything, what the fuck was that?
My cats are gone

once I was lying in my bed with my eyes closed and waiting for sleep…
I heard something said my name in low voice speak
the voice came right next to me, about a meter left
I frozen and I hold my breath
thrill hit me but I wasn't afraid
I was curious
What was it?
What's the meaning of this?
Did the voice come from inside of my head or was it something else?
I turned my head to the left and I opened my eyes
I didn't see anything
I rolled over, closed my eyes, and I didn't even want to look anymore

one night it happened again
a low voice called me by my name
just the same way as before, about a meter left
like a precise repeat breath
I looked, but I didn't see anything
I rolled over and fell asleep without a thing

the third time was a charm
the night was silent and dark
I was lying in my bed with my eyes closed and waiting for sleep...
when I felt a presence of something right above me
madness entered my mind
- should I open my eyes?

I opened my eyes and I was terrified
something was hovering above me in a golden smoke, looking at me
I frozed with anxiety, closed my eyes and took cover behind my arms
what the hell was going on?
Was it somekind of spirit, hallusination or was it just me going crazy?
I didn't want to open my eyes anymore and I hoped to fall asleep
I rolled over and fell asleep

the craziest, the weirdest...
and the most amazing thing...is that an experience of same sort has
earlier happened to my father

he saw a pharaoh

the real thing

but that's another story

THE SPIRIT OF LAHTI

We're leaving from the bar to walk towards the next bar
with me there's a 38-year old woman and a 33-year old man
I don't know them

. we're walking along the autumnal dark street when suddenly someone
attacks us from behind
– What the fuck are you doing?!
– You insult me
– What the fuck?! I've never even seen you! Who the fuck are you
anyway?!

The talk doesn't help
the bastard attacks again, but doesn't get a hit
I'm estimating the situation fast to end it
punch, get beaten or run
I have to handle this on my own

a couple of punches and the bastard takes a distance
I'll take a few steps and I'm giving a couple of punches more fist-dance
the bastard drops down
the cars are honking on long

from the ground I grab my stripped hoodie and I put it into my pocket
smoothly
the bastard gets up and his face is in blood
he doesn't attack anymore
better to end the score...before the cops are coming on
– Fuck off! We'll be on our way...

when we get into the bar I go to the counter to buy some lonkero
the saleswoman stares at my bloody fist but doesn't say anything, just
pouring lonkero
goes without saying
don't even ask while I'm paying...
my bowl of victory

you get what you pay for...
eventually

Welcome to Lahti

COLLATERAL REALITYS

One day when I was "meditating" I experienced something that is
difficult to understand
head full of electricity I peeked into the deep
I was present in five different worlds at the same time
sixth world was called the thinker of the mind

I was scared badly
sadly it was insane
I thought I was going to loose my brain
my consciousness was in a very unpleasant state
I was forced to find a getaway out of my rate

my mind was fucked up and I was trying to find myself
I used all my resources in focusing getting out of there
I struggled and regained control bit by bit
It wasn't a pleasant landing, it was a hit

I hardly want to go there ever again

It was a scary space...
a drain

DROPZONE

Strange mood, freaky feeling
common sense come to nothing
slow reactions, secret fixations
the disappearing presence

emptiness, bluntness, apathetic depression
all indifferent, meaningless
awareness fading, glassy eyes staring
inner mirrors are breaking into pieces

sleepy, dizzy, harmonic mind
Is this the art of the sandman of the night?

The doors are closed...
but the windows are opening
windows into space

consciousness trying to fight against the other world,
the dreamworld…
failuring it

control denied!

Irreversible blackout

the dropzone

THEM

I'm in a hall…
travelling without moving at all
floating backwards, going forward…
towards to the unknown zone

they are taking me…
making me hear the silence…
to see the surrounding seriousness…
making me feel the softness and safety…
taking care of me

bright lights, foggy lights looking nice
I'm alright, I don't fight this time
I let Them to take me, I want to let go
relax and go with the flow

I feel comfortable, calm and good
maybe happy, or just a fool
but I'm ready to see all that is true

all conception is in me
I love life, I love death

who's going to love me when I draw my final breath?

DREAMS

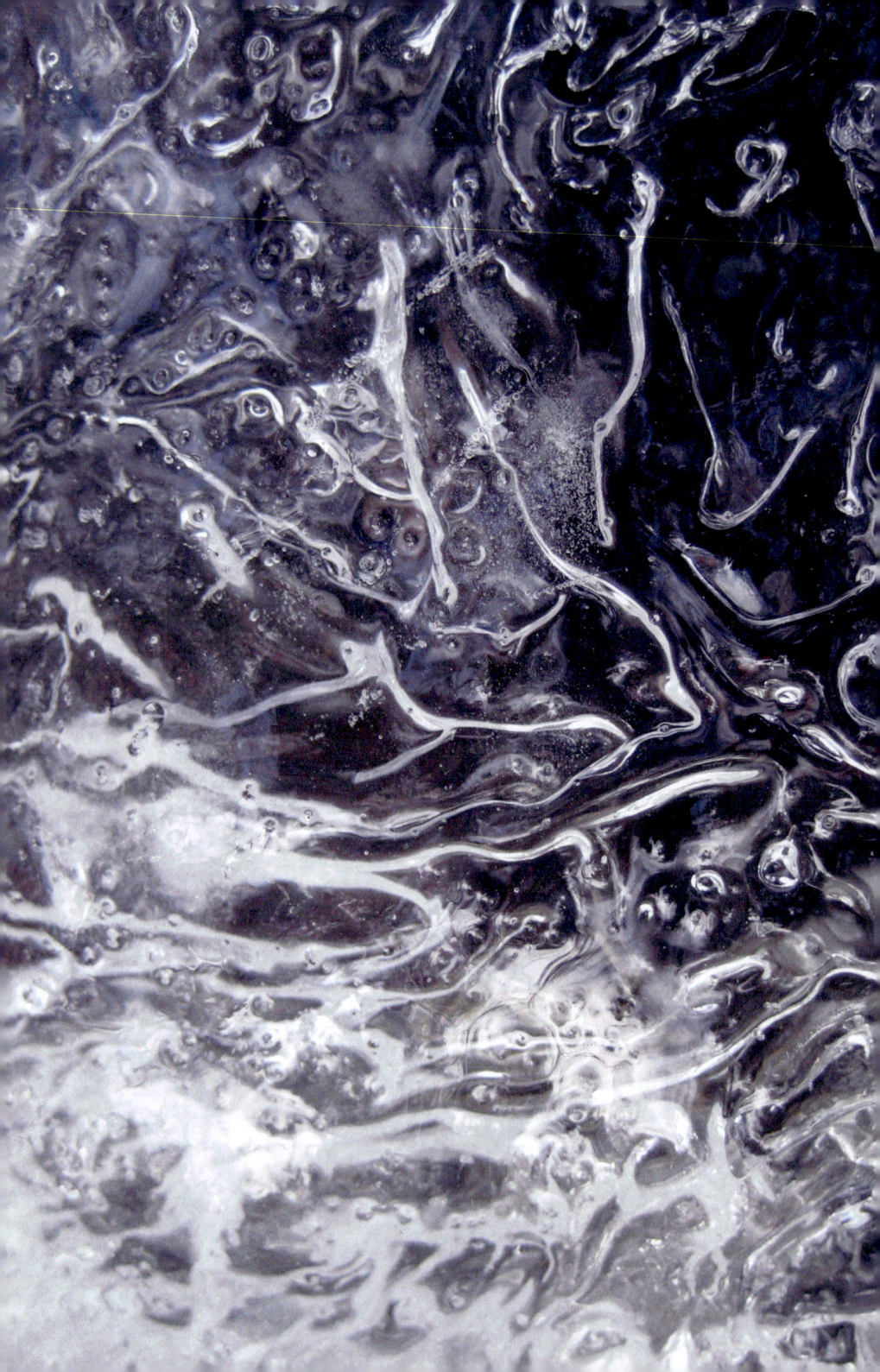

ASTRAL DREAM

In astral dream I'm diving into the Brazilian favela heat
I'm flying as a spirit and I'm exploring places, I'm exploring humans
and buildings
I see the ruins of the houses, shacks
I see dirt and poverty, homeless cats
I see hard life

people don't see me...
but they can hear me
they're not afraid at all...
and not really reacting when I tell them that I'm here in spirit form

they can even touch me, feel me...
but that doesn't amaze them either
they're not really paying attention to me
they just go on doing their own things, you see

that makes me meditative indeed

my unsubstantial astral body, my invisible spirit body
my aura
where do you guide me?
What does this all mean...
in astral dream?

THE NIGHT OF THE LIZARDS

I open the door into the room
on the bed is sitting a girl child, a prophet of doom
I don't see her face
I go sit next to her place

she behaves strangely, unnaturally...
and moaning like a cursed
she's fidgeting and laughing diabolically...
and trying to scare me at first

she's trying to overtake me
not working, I can see
I look at her and I say: "I eat your head."
I start to laugh because she's dead...
but still alive sickly, so sardonicly ill
I bite her head and the bones are crunching until...

(sigh)
I wake up drooling in total sweat

erm...so...like...what a fuck was that?

Bizarre wizard..,
in the night of the lizards

that's that

BLACKNESS

I'm in cold blackness
I feel the presence of evil in the darkness
obscure whisperings are breaking the dominant muteness
only light, the light of the flashing thunderstone starts to reveal a
horrible scene
in the black harsh environment, moving of the black unhuman beings

I'm frozen to the spot...
and I'm too afraid to move or breath
I'm in shock
I stare at the scene of horror with tears in my eyes...
and try to keep myself together, cause I fear of losing my mind
I feel like I'm going to die

I want to get out of here, I want this to end
anything but not this
I wish death
...
time stops

blackness swallows me into the black crowd and I scream
all the emotions and meanings are disappearing
no one hears, no more fears
aimless, sick rambling continues here

I notice that I belong to them
I'm the same
I'm a lost soul, black creature from hell...

in oblivion

Omnes est temporalis.

THANK YOU

Thanks: Jouni Huttu, Anni Kotiaho de Oliveira, Teemu Leskinen, Kirsi Tuulivirta, Juhapekka Jussi Jokelainen and of course BoD.